CAST IRON P(

THE ALCHEMIST'S DAUGHTER

SOPHIA ISABELLA MURRAY

Time is an Ocean Publications

Time is an Ocean Publications
An Imprint of **write***ahead*
Lonsdale Road
Wolverhampton WV3 0DY

First Printed Edition published
by **Time is an Ocean Publications 2022**
Text copyright © **Sophia Isabella Murray**
The Alchemist's Daughter is part
of the **Cast Iron Poetry** series
The right of Sophia Isabella Murray to be identified as the
author of this work has been asserted by her,
in accordance with the
Copyright, Designs and Patents Act 1988

**Books in the Cast Iron Poetry series
are all available from Amazon**

Reality Cornflakes
A Moon Magnetized This Screeching Bird
The Arbitrary Fractals of an Oracle
Sonnets
Minotaur and Other Poems
An Alpine State of Mind
Blue Note Poems
Echoes and Stardust
Under the Weight of Blue
In Pursuit of Dragonflies
An Escape to Stay
Addled Petals
Baker's Dozen
When the Party's Over
Spilling Earl Grey Tea on an Oriental Rug
Moonbeam-Sentinels & Sunbeam-Forgettance
John Clare's Troubled Grandson
Time Travels
We Grow in the Dark Like All Good Things
When Fold and Twine
From the River to the Sea
The Alchemist's Daughter

DEDICATION

To Mack, Genevieve, Rosie, Jonah - we
make a good team.
Also, to my partner Ed, who does not
understand poetry, yet continues to
pretend to understand what I am doing.
And to my coven of found sisters Becka,
Julie, Laura and Kim – you get me
With thanks to poetry feedback and
workshops from Amelia Louili and
Rebecca Green.

Preface

When I first met Sophia, she smiled with her eyebrows raised, reddish blonde curls around her Cheshire smile. "I thought you'd be tall!" she laughed.

We were immediate friends. While I am in fact inwardly 10 feet tall and bulletproof, the truth is the bulletproof vest of me is squeezed into 5'2" good girl who *"loves horses and America, too."*

We had met team teaching an online course, Rosie the Riveter hovering on the wall behind me; Sophia's grey-nosed dog Suzie punctuating post-modern poetry with her barks and stretches. We were a dream team, finding friendship in a time of Covid.

What I learned slowly but intensely about the writer of this collection over the last two years is this: She is the tall one. A humble giant.

Since that day we met, her words regularly launch me flailing across the ether into deep, cold rivers and then grab me by the shirt front and rattle every cage I have ever hidden in.

I have worked in education in three countries across three decades with students from more than 30 different nations and I have never met an educator who connected as empathically with students.

Sophia is an observer of life and she has eyes that see the unseen. You'd think that she had x-ray vision or psychic powers and, while she probably possesses both, her tools are simple. No crystal balls or gleaming keyboards but instead a campervan office in her driveway named Arthur, his wheels long hidden by overgrown patches of grass, scraps of paper and the nearest pen available.

Inside this makeshift office fringed with hippie beads and feminist mantras, the work in these pages came to life. One word at a time. At night, in the early morning, after long naps and through late nights, written to the rhythm of the relentless Northumberland rain, by hands warmed by hand knit fingerless gloves in a place heated by one single kettle on a square of Formica. Sophia's words are simple and profound, like nearly everything about her.

She doesn't announce herself or her talent but don't be fooled. Hers is the voice rising up in perfect time to point us all back to ourselves out of the ashes of Covid, conservative politics, and broken economies. Within minutes of meeting, she will know you. She will have noticed the slant of your smile from across the hall, the colour of your shoes, the way you accentuate a point in a higher pitch. And more than that, you will feel seen in these pages. In a time of isolation, you will feel seen and known and may it be a relief.

Emily Dickinson said, *"If I read a book [and] it makes my whole body so cold no fire can ever warm me, I know that is poetry. If I feel physically as if the top of my head were taken off, I know that is poetry. These are the only ways I know it. Is there any other way?"*

I suggest you get yourself a helmet and a good spot by the fireplace before you turn the page. Sophia Murray has the keys to your cage.

Kim Braschko Hoelterhoff

Contents

Moonless Earth Theory
A Drunken Portrait of my Family History
Cut scene from a repressed memory
For the Fir Tree That Lives in Me
The Alchemist's Daughter
The Museum of Past Selves
On the day of never
The Water Rises
Bride's Hall
Wishbone
Holding Space
The Vase
Jouska Polka
The Fatality of Introspection
Matchstick mouth
Investigation into self love
I refuse to join any club that would have me as a member
Collected Fragments of Broken Dreams
Digestive System of the Female Sea Serpent
Girl on top
Cuckoo Boy
STOP. PREVENT YOUR DEATH. GO NO FURTHER
Skinwalkers
Good Girls & Bad Girls (Madonnas and Whores)
Pink Moon Murder
The Little Mermaid Gets a Smear Test
Anthotype

A true story of how I came to be
How do you want us?
Dog Husband
Snake Wife
Lilith
The Red Woman
L'Appel du Vide
Erasure of a love letter to prove I can turn gold
into lead
Fawn chorus/Vows for a marriage
The Cloutie Tree
What Doesn't Kill You
My Therapist Said I Wear My Trauma So Lightly
Ochrewood
The Daughter speaks to the Devil
Becoming
And If I Am My Foot, I Am The Sun
Kintsugi Repair Kit

Moonless Earth Theory

A non-exhaustive list of the things that would happen if we blew up the moon:

1. A punctured skyline. Hidden stars uncovered by her jealous face. It is brighter now.
2. Constant movement. Calendar without crosses. The truth of 24 hours in a day.
3. Still waters. Smaller tides. Calm ripples to the shoreline. Make the crossing to the holy islands without a timetable.
4. Janus seasons. Half summer, half ice age. On the surface we are golden. Our shadows know our crime.
5. Blood without cause. Our red wedding ends in acrimonious divorce.

A Drunken Portrait of my Family History

Shhhhhhhhhhhhhhhhhhhhhhhh.

One side were all hatched from lapwing eggs
just off the ledge of the Tyne
Laid in an oyster shell by the sea captain's daughter:
a long line of water dwellers.
Up to our necks in brine.

The other side were never really born at all
Born in the caul, breathing if mother did.
Died in the same beds they arrived in.
Sisters waved them off on the quayside.
Torpedos had other ideas.

Only two were hit overall.
We've always been lucky that way.

John danced when Isabella took his ring.
Bought the house he was born in.
Dead John wasn't so lucky.
His ring was found in the bunk
under an unsent postcard to NYC.

Miss Henry found her mother dead in the morning.
Mother's shell cracked at 56.

Shhhhhhhhhhhhhhhhhhhhhhhh.

She ran away with the curly haired boy.

Miss Henry (she never took his name) never spoke
about that.
Came back to sleep in her mother's grave.
Hid tuna fish in the washing machine while
John now danced around invisible snakes.

Eric, the man with the curls Miss Henry envied
died in the shower. An unfinished cigarette by the
tub.

I was 11 months old. An unfinished granddaughter.
No one ever spoke about that.

Shhhhhhhhhhhhh.

I think sometimes they're all in here.
That's why mother never liked me.
I was the death in the bed.

Cut scene from a repressed memory

The feeling is there but the narrative is harder to hold onto.

HIM: You are evil.
> *You are not mine.*

> *I have lost you.*

> *You are broken glass in sand.*

SHE is walking up a hill wearing sunglasses on a day of rotten milk.

HIM: You cannot behave this way.
> *You are not what I made.*

> *I was planted & never grew.*

SHE is thinking of the safety of a green velvet armchair and white noise.

HIM: Don't ever say that. Don't ever. Ever say that.
> *I am afraid.*

> *Of your truth. Of life. The way you love.*

The script clicks. Like broken typewriter keys. They want to play. SHE is tired of being the madwoman in the portrait they all hang in their rogues' gallery.

For the Fir Tree That Lives in Me

Lying in the frames between my heart, living fir
Feeding on the wasted breath, the giving fir.

Forest skyline hinges on chiselled bone.
In dark pleural blooms feeding on light, unforgiving
fir.

Root meets bronchial fissures in unseen tissue
Life as two in one spirit song, singing fir.

In absence you grow volatile without sacrifice.
One more breath to aid the killing fir.

Hold this one a little longer, a little more.
Contractions twist in jest. Spitting fir.

The Alchemist's Daughter

Nigredo - The Blackening

She is a nightmare. She is all of their worst fears.
She sings and dances in the corner by the bamboo
bookcase.
She laughs uncontrollably at the words she doesn't
yet understand.
She runs but always comes back. The cave of the
chest carries their projector.
She is their unwitting screen.

Albedo - The Whitening

She is the script yet to be written. They are making
their mark.
She is told she has blotted her copybook. Around the
black spot
she sees the potential for more. Bleached hands wring
under fountains of praise for giving the right answers.
They taste wrong
in her mouth. Like the fresh gum of an absent milk
tooth.

Citrinitas - The Yellowing

The world is a terrible place. Home is safe. This
doesn't explain
the dread of the staircase. This is the stair where he
cried.

This is the stair she fell from. This is the stair where
she pissed herself.
This is the stair where the telephone lives.
Behind the downstairs door the ringing is dulled
so we can pretend not to hear it.
The outside world is a terrible place.

Rubedo - The Reddening

She learned about it too late. Transmutation.
We don't talk about it here. The outside is a terrible
place.
The Alchemist's face - a furious peony. There is no
cure for this. The black earth nightmare child woke
in a bed of red desert sand. Inextricably altered.
He grieves. Red is too close you see. We are made of
red.
How can they project onto what knows itself? There
is no cure for this.

The Museum of Past Selves

We open at one. Sharp.
Don't mind the guard.
She is sleeping on the job.
We're here to learn.

The Toddler - 1992 - clay on board

'She really wanted to be Mary.
Teddy Bear natural birth in the nursery.
An uncomfortable phone call home.'

Precocious Child - 1996 - paper cutting

'She always had an answer for everything.
A walking dictionary: English was easy.
Friends were not.'

Weird/Queer? - 2000 - sound installation

'A soundtrack no one cared for.
She kissed a boy once.
That came as a surprise to everyone.'

The Dropout - 2008/2011 - found objects

'Alcohol is not a suitable catalyst for learning.
Neither is pregnancy.
Free fall.'

The Mother - 2011 - woodblock print

'She has forgotten everything.
She remembers the shape of her own.
She is learning to keep everyone alive.'

Victim - 2015 - watercolour

'She still cannot breathe at the sight of a pink towel.
He flung it on the bed afterwards.
As if to cover *her* shame.'

Halfling - 2016 - mixed media

'One foot in the light.
Devils chained to yesterday and the day before.
In his eyes she sees she is not the evil one.'

Shadow and Body - 2022 - photograph

'She captured the dark.
It was not as terrifying as she had previously thought.
The image needs the negative for the whole picture.'

New exhibit coming soon.

On the Day of Never

From a cornfed tongue
Pulled cleanly from the ears
Get yourself to the fields where the pepper grows

                                             I will love you when
salt glows
                                             When a week is four
Thursdays

The rooster lays an egg
His mouth a snarl, spilling with teeth
Waiting for the larks to fall in cooked

Mother grabs her net by the door
To catch the wind & scoop up
Clams in the field

                                             I crunch the peppers
under the heel
                                             Watching the salt of
the egg timer swim up
                                             Waiting for the bulb
to glow

The Water Rises

A door.
Behind, a stack
of empty shells
cleaned by hand.
Wrapped in the sky -
spilled water colours.
A once painted black
wooden floor.
There's warmth here.
The water rises.

Once children laughed
Fathers taught sons
how to build castles
Mothers chided little ones
moving out of sight
warning them of danger
smearing skin with fables.
The water rises.

Shore line's soliloquy
interrupted rudely
by the tired rattling
of the bird in the cage
White bars against black
Feathered barcoded bird
Tagged once. Loved
then abandoned.
The water rises.

Once there was singing
Smiles crept over worried lines
when the men came home
They all sang songs while
the sun slipped behind.
Egg yolk broken in unsure hands
scattering shells on dry land.
The water rises.

Hips lower and legs
shrink under me
Sand piles between
disappearing claws
Bent knees struggle
staying still.
The water rises.

A voice I know
calls to her
in lullabies
this isn't the end
I scream to break
the rhythm of sleep
to the empty cage
filled with the clean picked
corkscrew shells.
The water rises.
The water rises.
The water rises.

Bride's Hall

The roses have asthma
and shouldn't exist in this
sick shade of flush
Dying brides on the altar
Of our windowsill

Molars are growing on the
sole of my boot &
I gnaw my way out
Feet first through concrete
Into mellow clay

We dressed it up in ceremony
Whether we cremate or bury
It is in our bones to honour it
Mama said no would marry me
No one would *ever* marry me.
In my spite I bathed in white lace
False peonies at my chest.

I line the aisle with the others
Psychic violence of the stained glass
pours its light onto our bodiced hearts.
A mannequined marriage
Marching to their tune.

Wishbone

the power of the wishbone
the bone itself
a revered female
made of iron

I wonder
breaking the wish of
merry thoughts
marriage bones
a second chance

hiding inside her closed fists
a lucky break

Holding Space

I've condemned the morning to delay
Contained another apocalypse
behind my tongue

Thumbs printed on my jawline
Bracelets of life break
over Adam's grounded fruit

This god is on mute

The Vase

Why do we pick the living
fresh from newly baptised soil
only to place them
in the same places
we keep the ashes of the dead?

Jouska Polka

Steps in
2/4
talking
to my
self as
if I
know what
to do

take one
step for-
ward one
step back
We don't
deserve
to move
We stick
here in
the mud

It all
might be
ok
one day

One day
never
comes here
Always

two-day
Not a
good day
One day

It can
be a
good day
If I
believe
it could

Even
Peter
Pan gave
it up
Got out
of bed

He had
something
to get
up for

Am I
the bad
voice still?
We are
safe here
We don't

need to
learn how
to fly

We are
stuck in
the mud

Stick in
the mud
and we
can't fail
can't fly
we can
just be

The Fatality of Introspection

'Hopelessness is a beautiful thing. It means you're not torturing yourself with the way things could have been' - Duncan Trussell

three eyes are undimmed
in a state beyond pain, you
hope to feel sad again.

Matchstick mouth

What does it mean
If when I dream of you
Asking if I still love you
All I can muster from
Under my tarred tongue is
A spent match?

Investigation into self-love

Right eye not as almond shaped as left. Left side is better. The genuine smile lies on the devil's side. Exhausting exercise. Minutes pass. There is less love here than before.

You cannot imitate yourself.

I refuse to join any club that would have me as a member
(After Groucho Marx)

junkies/genius
too much/too young
live fast/live loose
make a pretty corpse

a wise career move for some
I got the memo

made a reservation in February '16
got as far as the front desk
a rebellious heart
made other dinner plans

Collected Fragments of Broken Dreams

I am lost in alleyways by canals that stripe the land
Aisles for the open procession
of industrial smog
it canters over every surface
flesh / metal

I am on the edge of the universe
tearing open the sun to eat
the fruit it births with
sweet seeds that burst
supernovas under my tongue

I am falling from a building
I can't remember opening the door to
catching sparrows in my hands
that only now stop singing

I am standing on her stairs
in the home I had forgotten
with the smell of her soap
still on my hands
I inhale. I remember.

I am in the pine forest
Trees hold the faces of a past life.
They tell me I should fall so deeply
in love I cannot see my own reflection.

I am barefoot in shallow water

Veiled hands beneath
Grasping at my heels
I can join them for the dawn chorus.

I am at sea, my thighs itch.
A crash of timpani drums
sending splinters in the air
they never land, frozen on the canvas
you rest the brush between your teeth.

I am buried under white linen
with the grey stone above me.
Fingernails holding on to my name
I pull my body from broken dreams.

Digestive System of the Female Sea Serpent

pulled past
   pegged teeth
     engorged tongue
       swollen lips
         scuffed shoes
           left on the shore
           pushing deep towards
       the rippling crush
      the anticipation
       -fullness
      he calls
        to the behind
         of her tongue
          the heat of her belly
        starting at his toes
         he dances
          she dances
     swallowing hard
     the joy
      the gorge
       the full belly
        the heartbeat within
         next to her own
          darkness within
        swimming into
   a crescendo of waves
       she rests

Girl on top

Astride the beautiful terrors of eternity
She on top
He, hard granite
Repulsed by himself
Commands the ravens
To grasp her wrists
She whistles
Wrist bones anchored to a countertop
Askew
She, askance, spits at gravity
He ripples
Fighting buckling knees
Begging the cobra to bite
She kisses
The air, blue eyed
Cobra and breath strike
To meet
Her lips
Stealing seeds
Between the dam of
Her lips
To come in paradise
Touching orchids
That we know will die so soon
She runs forefingers over
The dragon's kiss
To come in paradise
To leave paradise
On top.

Cuckoo Boy

our cuckoo will sing at midnight
the hand of the clock thinks about it

dimples frame my spine in honour of Venus
tailbone shifts, sensing sunlight

petals ripening against
a sun and moon embracing

over primordial waters
in you I am resurrected

you grew in mud, planting roots
in contaminated waters yet

you are unstained
you bloom in tears

baptising the fruit planted
by the cuckoo bird song

STOP. PREVENT YOUR DEATH. GO NO FURTHER

Play out the rest of this catastrophe in the kopfkino.
I've booked a seat for two at the matinee.
Fatally flawed to keep breathing.
Thanks to the parasite that made a home
At the top of my spine.
 It just wants
To keep living.
It just wants
To find answers.

I'm not here to make you happy
I'm here to keep you alive

She **will** tire, we are certain
Grey pillared temples
Behind shared eyes
We'll watch our hands crumble

Skinwalkers

We are ghosts
Eating ghost food
Outside of ourselves
In the green room watching
The players play
far too seriously

Good Girls & Bad Girls
(Madonnas and Whores)

Let me kneel   Beside you I get
down and pray.   hot chamber bells ringing.
Give myself to   myself? I love myself. Oh
you Lord   sing to my skin.
I have no   desire, fuck this devil out,
Power   through self-taught scripts
I am your   naughty, angel, baby, girl, mother
vessel in blue   keeper of womanhood
I will not   do as you are told.
Touch   the edge of sainthood,
the forbidden,   is out of reach.

Pink Moon Murder

Spiteful clots drape down like melting wax
on pristine porcelain

As she blossoms
I shed now useless skin

Another branch lost:
pruned from the family tree

Sanguine fluid fills cardboard cups
Pervasive disintegration

I am the victim but not the corpse
I am the murderer but not the cause

Budding belly in the sky taunts me
with what we could have been.

The Little Mermaid Gets a Smear Test

*(or things I didn't realise I'd have to deal with when I thought
I was a mermaid)*

Cold bed. Rough and ready paper bedspread.
This is not part of the fairytale.
Feet glued at the heels.

She can't see what horrors sit beside The Doctor.
Nothing like a prince.
Trying to be charming.

A fairy godmother beside him.
Smiling but looking long past
between her eyes not in them

Nothing to worry about here dear
Just let me know if you're in any discomfort
Be over in a jiffy

Staring at ceiling tiles.
Sheathed in scales.
She can't see where hands go.

The godmother called it what?
a specula - *whatsamijigger*.
She lies back -
remembers a bad dream about Sebastian.

Anthotype

A lemon peel crown sits where I once saw your face.
Bathing at midnight, the contradictions take shape.
Oak knotted hands reach out to catch nothing from
the vapours
dying away with each rapid blink.

Thrum humming lights.
Thrum hummm buzz behind the eyes.
Nightwater orchids. Clublight dancers.
The monastery of our bedsheets.
Imprinted on the threshold of sleep.
A reverse memory.
Drifting into the vacuum behind

A true story of how I came to be

Free form sugar skull branded in copper cat gut curls
Driftwood spine set with shards of sea glass
I'm a collector/collection of things they thought
They'd lost at sea

Swaddled in fleece snagged on Tansy
Snapped onto self before the Cinnabar moths make a
home
Plucked a tic for each eye
Bloodsucker starved of I
Feeds on - what must they think of me?

Spoiled crab apple core in the heart of me
We share bites. Kerosene kisses.
Sick up seeds into the flames we kept tame.
I build myself from dirt without permission

How do you want us?

Like bitches we should feel the earth
with the palms of our hands
Breaking the eggshells with callouses
so the witches are anchored & craftless

Like the spider we should unravel silk
in only the safest places
Feasting on the man that feeds us
The gentle hammock of the lingering unborn

Like hornets they have learned
Not to speak our name -
lest we sting & burn the soles of their feet -
We hum our elegy to their deaf ears.

Dog Husband

He is of the earth
He has gained the trust
of every path he forged
He bled an oath to the woods
to the trees
Now he walks
Comfortably blind

He bares his teeth to
unknown threats
He dreams of the wolf
The moon, a beacon of history.

He loved a pig once.
He learned from his mistake.
He is fearful of loving again.

Snake Wife

She is of the earth.
She does not trust it
against the belly she drags along.
She is occupied enough with
nightfall and earthshine.
She moves in the space between.
Comfortably blind.

She bares her fangs
Every *thing* is a threat
She dreams of hunger filled;
the moon an egg to be devoured.

She wants to love.
She has only just survived.
She wants more than this.

Lilith

The Night Bird told me
stop overriding your truth

hidden under a false tooth
like a delicious pill
to pop
bite clean in half
letting ill conceived poison
spill over gums

Kill the desperate need
To be loved
By everyone
To be shrunk down
To fit into his palm

We are broken yolks
spilling into her nest
Free from the lie of him

The Red Woman

We gather sleep
holy and revered
absence of being
We sever the sinful pride
of living
We take everything
too hot to touch and too cold to save
while the rest flows
into the spaces one holds
when in the arms of another.

Madness thrives in your absence
and I reason with the fear
and want
to be safe
to be loved
married to a purpose

The lamb at the altar and
the wolf at the door
I graze absentmindedly
in ignorance
Peacefully
side by
side.

L'Appel du Vide

The taste of you
is like the split
second thought of
walking into
oncoming traffic

Your mouth calls me to the void

Erasure of a Love Letter to Prove I can Turn Gold into Lead

                                                        I

                                      believe

                                                       I

                                    'm in
                                    your

        past   writing from
                 another
realm.   In the dream
place   you
                                   are mad.

                        Sitting,

chewing my   silly mask

A   nightmare

        A moment   to

doubt   my

        love

Fawn Chorus/Vows for a Marriage

I want to do the job your lungs do so well
Crushed against the grain of your bones
Strapped to the rib cage
safely intertwined with sinew
Defying the pull
with you
in you
burning up every inch of me

The Cloutie Tree

Was everything to me for years
I buried their hearts there
Cut my fingers to prove my grief
Seven knuckles cut to the quick

Her face painted on a bauble
Wrapped in red cords I knotted
Sealed with wax on a forgiving new moon
This is just a love letter to my enemy
I love my enemy
Who else can I hate?

Black soot salt unknotted at the roots
Pickled unthinkables hung from branches
As they rot, we heal

What Doesn't Kill You

makes that pound of flesh scab over into a delicious
itch in the back of your chest at 3am; makes you
wander around your own home as if the dead are
waiting behind each closed door with *I told you so's*;
makes you stare lightyears past the familiar faces
asking the same magnolia questions every day; makes
you search for the one micro expression that you can
use as an excuse to yourself to never look at them
again; makes you crumple your love into paper
aeroplanes, launched into thunderstorms so every
passenger is lost at sea; makes you pick pick pick pick
away at your reflection until the shards fill your palms
with silver, Judas is what they called you anyway;
makes you wonder just whose voice that is in your
head, this isn't my narrative so then to whom does it
belong; makes you wake up to empty popped plastic
and bloody sheets, lambasting the English language
because words can't cover this; makes you think
you're failing because survival should have made you
superwoman, not this, this nuclear disaster; makes
you wish they had seen the white flag go up on day
one and claimed their triumphs then and there,
planting their victory banner on your grave; makes
you realise that all the things said and done didn't
make you stronger, you did.

My Therapist said I Wear My Trauma So Lightly

Like talcum powder
I ground up the memories
dust them over my torso
hung off the clavicle

A daily ritual
makes the foundation
a clean slate
for the ashes of today

Silt builds with progress
altering the course
the unseen load beneath
steady rippling flow

Ochrewood

She said
I was a beautiful person
The compliment died in the air
like a struck moth
before it could land
Grey ash on the bottle green armchair

She said
She was sorry
that happened
and to breath through it
Let the sadness come
The self-immolation just
a scorch mark at her door

The Daughter speaks to the Devil

(After Rebecca Tamás)

I think I'm in the wrong

I don't

But really I'm sure I should be

You are right where you put yourself

I thought I'd

Did you ever stop to think?

Well, I did as I was

And that is precisely the problem

But. But I never caused any

And look where it got you

I'm sorry but I really think there's been

We don't do those here

I want to talk to the person in charge

Speaking

You're

Not what you expected

I thought

You thought the primroses on the tor were perfect too
I'm the worms beneath and I make the ground thrive

But aren't you

Black suited and booted bitch
We all like to call Her her
They forget we can bad too

I think I

Forgot to crack the eggshells
And craft your own path

Well it never seemed

Threading the needle without a tongue
Never lets a stitch get sewn

There was that time

The oldest tree in the world is still petrified
Neither here nor there

Maybe this could be

It's hard to be wrong when you have my sense of conviction.

Should I

What size boots do you take?

Becoming
(The Body of a Woman)

Curl the seed out from behind your tonsils; relieve
the itch with forked tongues. Fill the garden with
peach trees; make the air sweet, let it possess you. Dig
a hand span down into the earth beside the roots.
Place yourself here. Work the black grit beneath your
toenails. Let the insects scuttle around the hair on
your feet. This is disgust; keep it buried. Smear the
soil up the back of your legs, between your legs, clod
it forcefully to your hips. It will stick here well. This is
growth; tend to it. Take a peach; bite. Chew with your
mouth open. Let the nectar rinse down the channel
of your collarbone, your breasts, your ribs, let it hang
from your pelvic bone. It is sticky, sweet, and cloying.
It is growth. It is blooming. The bees will come. This
is beauty, remember it.

And If I Am My Foot, I Am the Sun
(After Alan Watts)

If I am my foot, I am also the sun
If I am these four stakes steady in the mud
I am the light above

If I am rooted into the ground
If I am truly on my feet
I am exuberant with heat
I am my foot, I am the sun

Alchemy: a definition

Medieval; concerned with the transmutation of
matter into something of worth; the babe is
something to be sculpted; in her image; in her eyes all
that glitters is certainly not gold unless her hands are
upon it; unless she can hold a feather in her fist
against the weighted cries of the coarse stone and
both defy outside forces; the magick of wanting more
than there ever could be

Kintsugi Repair Kit

keep the broken body/she is beautiful/
will be beautiful/the flaws have their own landscape
across freckled skin/gold laces tied on her wrists/
golden lattice on the forearms/embrace the
imperfection/
golden stitches from the root to sacrum/meld the
tears
with molten gold/renewed she is a jewel/repaired she
is divine

About the Author

Sophia Isabella Murray is 10% witch, 10% poet, 10% hermit and 100% mother. She is also not very good at Mathematics so tries to use her words instead.

During a prolonged stay indoors along with the rest of the world, she decided to put the ukulele down and just write the lyrics; someone kindly informed her it was actually called poetry.

Sophia is terrified of and fascinated with the dark. She explores the twisted, tangled and uncanny feelings of trying to be a relatively decent human being in a world where most of the time something or someone (usually our own mangled ego) is out to destroy us.

She lives with her husband, children and her familiar - assuming the form of a small, angry terrier - in a house on the ley lines surrounded by the stormy Northumberland hills.

Sophia has been published in various anthologies by ***Blood Moon Poetry Press, Mum Poem Press, Sunday Mornings at the River, Bent Key, The 6ress and Free Verse Revolution Lit.*** This is her first collection.

You can view her work online at Instagram: **@sim_poetry**